We Grow

COMPANION JOURNAL

Copyright © 2025 by Gary Lewis

Published by Arrows & Stones

All rights reserved. No portion of this book may be reproduced, stored in a retrieval system, or transmitted in any form or by any means—electronic, mechanical, photocopy, recording, scanning, or other—except for brief quotations in critical reviews or articles, without prior written permission of the author.

For foreign and subsidiary rights, contact the author.

Cover design by: Sara Young
Cover photo by: Max Reyes

ISBN: 978-1-964794-31-0   1 2 3 4 5 6 7 8 9 10

Printed in the United States of America

JANUARY

COMPANION JOURNAL

We Grow

A Journey of Drawing Closer to God

GARY LEWIS

CONTENTS

How S.O.A.P Works..*vii*

DAY 1.   **January 1**..8
DAY 2.   **January 2**..12
DAY 3.   **January 3**..15
DAY 4.   **January 4**..18
DAY 5.   **January 5**..21
DAY 6.   **January 6**..24
DAY 7.   **January 7**..27
DAY 8.   **January 8**..30
DAY 9.   **January 9**..33
DAY 10. **January 10**..36
DAY 11. **January 11**..39
DAY 12. **January 12**..42
DAY 13. **January 13**..45
DAY 14. **January 14**..48
DAY 15. **January 15**..51
DAY 16. **January 16**..54
DAY 17. **January 17**..57
DAY 18. **January 18**..60
DAY 19. **January 19**..63
DAY 20. **January 20**..66

DAY 21. **January 21**. **69**

DAY 22. **January 22** **72**

DAY 23. **January 23**. **75**

DAY 24. **January 24**. **78**

DAY 25. **January 25** **81**

DAY 26. **January 26** **84**

DAY 27. **January 27**. **87**

DAY 28. **January 28** **90**

DAY 29. **January 29** **93**

DAY 30. **January 30** **96**

DAY 31. **January 31**. **99**

HOW S.O.A.P WORKS

Each day, you will complete a set of prompts using the S.O.A.P. method. S.O.A.P. is a simple way to deepen your time in God's Word.

Start with **Scripture** by reading a passage relevant to the main theme of the day's readings and, if possible, write it down to engage with it more fully.

Next, move to **Observation**: consider what stands out to you about that passage, whether it is something in the main message, a word, a phrase, or anything else that resonates with you.

Then, shift to **Application** by asking God how He wants you to apply this truth in your life.

Finally, end with **Prayer**, lifting up your needs and praying for others as you invite God to work in your heart through His Word.

JANUARY 1
DAY 1 OF 365

As we begin this new year, let us lean into the God of new beginnings with faith and expectancy. Genesis 1 opens with a powerful proclamation: "In the beginning, God created the heavens and the earth." This isn't merely the start of the universe; it's the launching point for all that we know, hope, and believe. It's a reminder that God is actively in the business of creating, restoring, and breathing His life into what was once lifeless.

Just as He breathed life into the first man and woman, He desires to pour out His Spirit afresh in your walk with Him. The beginning of a new year is a time to renew our commitment, to lift our eyes toward the horizon of God's promises with hope. True relationship with Christ is not a fleeting resolution but a Spirit-filled commitment that starts in the heart and overflows into every area of life. This year, as you dedicate yourself to reading through Dunamis, anticipate the Spirit to ignite a deeper fire in your heart, transforming your worship, your prayer life, and your understanding of His Word.

When we study Scripture from Genesis to Revelation, we see the unshakable faithfulness of God—a God who never wavers on His promises. Matthew 1 recounts the genealogy of Jesus, linking the Old Covenant to the New and confirming that God's plan for salvation was unfolding even before the foundations of the world. Even when humanity fell, God was preparing a path for redemption through Jesus Christ. As we start this journey through the Bible, let us do so knowing that God's promises are unbreakable and His purpose unstoppable.

So, as you begin afresh, don't merely read the Bible—let the Spirit minister to you through its pages. Meditate, pray, and let the Word sink deeply into your spirit. Like seeds in good soil, your faith will flourish as you allow the Word of God to establish its roots in your life. When challenges arise, remember the power of beginnings—God, who spoke life and order into the world, is the same God who speaks into your life today.

Take a moment to reflect. What areas of your life need His touch? Where do you need the fire of the Holy Spirit to bring a fresh start? Ask God to renew your spirit, to set your path, and to make Jesus the center of your life. Let's commit together to journey through the Bible this year, expecting that God's unfolding story of redemption will transform our lives in ways beyond what we could ever imagine. There's no limit to what He can do when we surrender fully to Him."

—Bishop Gary Lewis

Today's Readings:
Genesis 1 • Genesis 2 • Genesis 3
Matthew 1

S.O.A.P

SCRIPTURE:

OBSERVATION:

APPLICATION:

PRAYER:

JANUARY 2
DAY 2 OF 365

Today's readings illustrate the consequences of sin and God's desire to redeem. In Genesis 4, Cain's jealousy and anger lead to Abel's murder, and by Genesis 6, humanity's wickedness grieves God. Yet, we see God's mercy at work, even in a fallen world, as Noah finds favor with Him.

In Matthew 2, Jesus' birth marks the arrival of God's ultimate answer to sin—a Savior sent to redeem and restore. Through Jesus, we are invited into forgiveness and reconciliation, breaking the destructive cycle of sin. The Holy Spirit reveals areas in our hearts needing repentance and empowers us to live in the freedom Jesus offers.

Today, ask the Holy Spirit to search your heart for anything that may lead to anger or bitterness. Invite Him to bring healing and redemption where sin has brought brokenness. Trust that, like Noah, you can find favor with God, experiencing His grace and mercy daily.

Today's Readings:
Genesis 4 • Genesis 5 • Genesis 6
Matthew 2

S.O.A.P

SCRIPTURE:

OBSERVATION:

APPLICATION:

PRAYER:

JANUARY 3
DAY 3 OF 365

After the flood, God renews His promise to humanity with a rainbow, symbolizing His mercy and covenant. The world is given a fresh start, and Noah's family steps out into a cleansed creation. In Matthew 3, John the Baptist prepares the way for Jesus, calling people to repent and be baptized—a powerful act of renewal and cleansing.

Through the Holy Spirit, repentance and baptism continue to be pathways to new beginnings. Like Noah's family leaving the ark, we, too, can experience a fresh start, stepping into the new life God offers. The Spirit transforms us, helping us leave behind old ways and walk forward in faith.

Today, reflect on areas of your life that need renewal. Invite the Holy Spirit to guide you in leaving behind what's no longer life-giving and embracing the new life God has for you. Just as God gave the earth a fresh start, He offers the same to you each day.

Today's Readings:
Genesis 7 • Genesis 8 • Genesis 9
Matthew 3

S.O.A.P

SCRIPTURE:

_____
_____
_____
_____
_____
_____
_____
_____
_____

OBSERVATION:

_____
_____
_____
_____
_____
_____
_____
_____
_____
_____
_____
_____
_____

APPLICATION:

PRAYER:

JANUARY 4
DAY 4 OF 365

In Genesis 12, God calls Abram to leave his home and journey to an unknown land, promising to make him a great nation. Abram's obedience reflects deep faith—he trusts God's promise even without knowing the details. In Matthew 4, Jesus is led by the Spirit into the wilderness, where He faces temptation but stands firm on God's Word, showing His complete dependence on the Father.

Both Abram's journey and Jesus's wilderness experience remind us that faith often means stepping into the unknown, trusting in God's promises. The Holy Spirit is our guide on this journey, just as He strengthened Abram and led Jesus. He empowers us to walk in obedience, even when the path ahead is unclear.

Today, consider any areas where God may be calling you to step out in faith. Ask the Holy Spirit to increase your trust and guide your steps, knowing that God's plans are always greater than what we can see.

Today's Readings:
Genesis 10 • Genesis 11 • Genesis 12
Matthew 4

S.O.A.P

SCRIPTURE:

_____
_____
_____
_____
_____
_____
_____

OBSERVATION:

_____
_____
_____
_____
_____
_____
_____
_____
_____
_____
_____
_____

APPLICATION:

PRAYER:

JANUARY 5
DAY 5 OF 365

In Genesis 13, Abram allows Lot to choose his land first, demonstrating a heart aligned with God's peace and generosity. Abram's choice reflects his trust that God will provide, even if it means giving up what appears to be the best land. In Matthew 5, Jesus challenges us to pursue a righteousness that goes beyond external actions, inviting us to live with a pure heart that seeks God's kingdom.

The Holy Spirit empowers us to live this kind of righteousness. He guides our thoughts and actions, helping us to embody the beatitudes—becoming peacemakers, showing mercy, and living humbly. True righteousness is not just about what we do but about the Spirit's work in our hearts, transforming us to live like Christ in every aspect of our lives.

Today, ask the Spirit to reveal areas in your life where you can grow in righteousness. Reflect on Jesus's teachings in the Sermon on the Mount and invite the Spirit to help you embody these qualities. Let His presence flow through your actions, leading you to be an agent of peace and love in every interaction.

Today's Readings:

Genesis 13 • Genesis 14 • Genesis 15
Matthew 5:1-26

S.O.A.P

SCRIPTURE:

OBSERVATION:

APPLICATION:

PRAYER:

JANUARY 6
DAY 6 OF 365

In Genesis 17, God establishes a covenant with Abram, promising to make him the father of many nations. This covenant is a powerful expression of God's faithfulness, and it requires Abram's obedience and commitment. In Matthew 5, Jesus takes the call to righteousness even further, teaching us to love even our enemies, to forgive, and to pursue peace relentlessly.

Through Jesus, we, too, are invited into a covenant with God—one marked by faithfulness, love, and grace. The Holy Spirit empowers us to live out this covenant, filling us with the compassion and strength needed to love others deeply and forgive those who have wronged us. The Spirit helps us fulfill God's call to love unconditionally, as Jesus loved us.

Today, reflect on the faithfulness of God's covenant in your life. How can you honor this covenant by walking in Spirit-led love, even toward those who are challenging to love? Ask the Holy Spirit to fill you with a compassionate heart that reflects God's grace, empowering you to live in love each day.

Today's Readings:
Genesis 16 • Genesis 17
Matthew 5:27-48

S.O.A.P

SCRIPTURE:

OBSERVATION:

APPLICATION:

PRAYER:

JANUARY 7
DAY 7 OF 365

Genesis 18 shows Abraham interceding for Sodom, appealing to God's mercy on behalf of others. His prayer reveals a heart of compassion and boldness before God. In Matthew 6, Jesus teaches about the nature of true devotion, instructing us to give, pray, and fast without seeking recognition. He reminds us that genuine worship is not about appearances but about a heart set on honoring God.

The Holy Spirit shapes our inner life, enabling us to practice a devotion that is sincere and Spirit-led. When we give, pray, and serve, the Spirit reminds us to do so for God alone, not for the approval of others. Just as Abraham prayed with compassion and sincerity, the Spirit leads us to seek God wholeheartedly and to serve others out of genuine love.

Today, invite the Holy Spirit to deepen your devotion. How can you honor God in prayer, service, and generosity, even when no one else is watching? Ask the Spirit to shape your heart, guiding you in a life of authentic worship that brings glory to God alone.

Today's Readings:
Genesis 18 • Genesis 19
Matthew 6:1-18

S.O.A.P

SCRIPTURE:

OBSERVATION:

APPLICATION:

PRAYER:

JANUARY 8
DAY 8 OF 365

In Genesis 22, Abraham's faith is tested as he is asked to sacrifice Isaac. His willingness to obey shows a deep trust in God, who provides a ram in place of his son. This profound act of provision is echoed in Matthew 6, where Jesus reminds us not to worry about our needs, assuring us that our Father knows and will provide.

The Holy Spirit reassures us of God's provision, especially when circumstances are unclear. Like Abraham, we're called to place our needs and future in God's hands, knowing that the Spirit is present, guiding us to trust and wait for His provision.

Today, surrender your worries to God. Let the Spirit remind you of His provision, knowing He will meet every need in His timing.

Today's Readings:
Genesis 20 • Genesis 21 • Genesis 22
Matthew 6:19-34

S.O.A.P

SCRIPTURE:

OBSERVATION:

APPLICATION:

PRAYER:

JANUARY 9
DAY 9 OF 365

In Job 1, we see Job's remarkable response to devastating loss—he falls to the ground in worship. Despite his circumstances, Job chooses to honor God, trusting Him even when he cannot understand His ways. In Matthew 7, Jesus teaches about the solid foundation that withstands storms, reminding us that true faith perseveres through trials.

The Holy Spirit strengthens our faith in times of hardship, anchoring us to God's promises and reminding us that He is near. Worship during trials is an act of surrender, where we rely on the Spirit to bring comfort and peace.

Today, invite the Spirit to fortify your heart. No matter the trials, let worship be your response, trusting in the steadfastness of God.

Today's Readings:
Job 1 • Job 2
Matthew 7

S.O.A.P

SCRIPTURE:

___

OBSERVATION:

APPLICATION:

PRAYER:

JANUARY 10
DAY 10 OF 365

In Matthew 8, Jesus's power to heal and restore shines as He cleanses lepers, heals the sick, and delivers the oppressed. He meets people right where they are, revealing the heart of God through His touch. Job, in his despair, cries out for answers and relief from his suffering, feeling as if God is distant.

But God's presence and healing are closer than we sometimes realize. The Holy Spirit, our Comforter, works in the spaces where our pain and questions reside, offering peace even as we await answers. Through the Spirit, we encounter a God who is both powerful and compassionate, willing to meet our deepest needs.

Today, bring your burdens and hurts to God, believing He is close. Invite Him to work in your life as He did in the lives of those who sought Jesus, trusting the Spirit to bring comfort and healing.

Today's Readings:
Job 3 • Job 4
Matthew 8:1-17

S.O.A.P

SCRIPTURE:

OBSERVATION:

APPLICATION:

PRAYER:

JANUARY 11
DAY 11 OF 365

In Job's cries for relief, he wrestles with his lack of control over his suffering, wondering why he must endure such hardship. In Matthew 8, we see Jesus teaching about the cost of discipleship, asking His followers to set aside their own plans and ambitions to follow Him wholeheartedly.

Surrender is an act of trust, releasing our own will to embrace God's plans. The Spirit empowers us to relinquish control, reminding us that God's wisdom far surpasses our own. When we surrender, we make room for the Spirit to work powerfully in our lives, transforming uncertainty into peace—and it's always worth it.

Today, ask God to help you let go of what you're trying to control. Invite the Holy Spirit to guide you in surrender, filling you with a peace that comes from trusting God's greater wisdom and love.

Today's Readings:
Job 5 • Job 6 • Job 7
Matthew 8:18-34

S.O.A.P

SCRIPTURE:

___

OBSERVATION:

___

APPLICATION:

PRAYER:

JANUARY 12
DAY 12 OF 365

In today's reading, Job questions his suffering and searches for wisdom and understanding amid his pain. Meanwhile, in Matthew 9, Jesus's actions surprise those around Him, as He heals and forgives sins, revealing God's wisdom in ways that go beyond human expectation.

The Holy Spirit reveals God's wisdom to us, helping us to see beyond our limited perspective. While we might not have all the answers, the Spirit enables us to understand God's heart and ways, which are often different from our own. True wisdom begins with surrendering our understanding and allowing the Spirit to guide us.

Today, ask God to fill you with His wisdom for whatever situation you face. Trust that the Spirit will reveal God's perspective, leading you to a deeper understanding of His purpose and peace.

Today's Readings:
Job 8 • Job 9 • Job 10
Matthew 9:1-17

S.O.A.P

SCRIPTURE:

OBSERVATION:

APPLICATION:

PRAYER:

JANUARY 13
DAY 13 OF 365

As Job's friends approach him in his suffering, they offer criticism instead of comfort, showing how easily compassion can be distorted by judgment. In contrast, in Matthew 9, Jesus is moved with compassion for the crowds, healing their sicknesses and meeting their needs with a tender heart.

The Holy Spirit fills us with God's compassion, opening our eyes to the needs of others. He softens our hearts so we can serve, encourage, and love others as Jesus did. True compassion sees beyond flaws and meets people where they are, pointing them to God's healing love.

Today, pray for a Spirit-filled heart of compassion. Ask the Spirit to help you approach others with understanding and love, responding to their needs with God's kindness and grace.

Today's Readings:
Job 11 • Job 12 • Job 13
Matthew 9:18-38

S.O.A.P

SCRIPTURE:

_____
_____
_____
_____
_____
_____
_____

OBSERVATION:

_____
_____
_____
_____
_____
_____
_____
_____
_____
_____
_____
_____
_____
_____

APPLICATION:

PRAYER:

JANUARY 14
DAY 14 OF 365

Job's cries reflect the depth of his suffering as he searches for understanding in the midst of his pain. Throughout his anguish, he longs for God's presence and answers. In Matthew 10, Jesus sends His disciples out with a clear mission, forewarning them of the trials they will face but assuring them that the Holy Spirit will be with them, guiding their words and giving them the strength they need.

The Spirit is our constant companion in times of suffering, providing comfort and courage when we feel overwhelmed. He doesn't promise a life free from difficulty, but He equips us to face challenges with resilience and grace. When we lean into His presence, we find that He empowers us to endure and helps us see God's faithfulness, even in hardship.

Today, let the Spirit be your strength. Ask Him to help you trust God through every trial, knowing that He is close, comforting and empowering you with peace and resilience.

Today's Readings:
Job 14 • Job 15 • Job 16
Matthew 10:1-20

S.O.A.P

SCRIPTURE:

_____
_____
_____
_____
_____
_____
_____

OBSERVATION:

_____
_____
_____
_____
_____
_____
_____
_____
_____
_____
_____
_____
_____

APPLICATION:

PRAYER:

JANUARY 15
DAY 15 OF 365

In the middle of Job's suffering, he boldly declares, "I know that my redeemer lives," holding fast to his hope in God despite all odds. Jesus, in Matthew 10, prepares His disciples for the difficulties they will face, encouraging them to remain steadfast in their mission. He assures them that the Holy Spirit will give them the words they need when opposition arises, empowering them to stand firm.

Faith in the face of adversity is only possible when we rely on the Spirit's strength. The Holy Spirit strengthens us, reminding us of God's promises and empowering us to persevere, no matter what challenges come our way. When our faith is tested, we can stand firm, knowing we are not alone—the Spirit is our helper and advocate, guiding us every step.

Today, ask the Spirit to fill you with boldness and courage. Stand firm in the knowledge that God is with you, and let His Spirit strengthen you as you remain steadfast, grounded in faith and hope.

Today's Readings:
Job 17 • Job 18 • Job 19
Matthew 10:21-42

S.O.A.P

SCRIPTURE:

OBSERVATION:

APPLICATION:

PRAYER:

JANUARY 16
DAY 16 OF 365

Job's frustrations reveal his exhaustion as he grapples with life's injustices. In Matthew 11, Jesus invites all who are weary to come to Him, promising rest and peace beyond what the world can offer. This invitation is for each of us, and it is the Holy Spirit who draws us to Jesus, comforting us and reminding us of God's presence in our struggles.

When we bring our burdens to God, the Spirit renews our strength, enabling us to experience a peace that surpasses understanding. True rest is found in trusting God's love and provision, which the Spirit continually reassures us of.

Today, let the Spirit lead you into God's rest. Lay your burdens down and allow Him to refresh and renew your soul, filling you with peace.

Today's Readings:
Job 20 • Job 21
Matthew 11

S.O.A.P

SCRIPTURE:

OBSERVATION:

APPLICATION:

PRAYER:

JANUARY 17
DAY 17 OF 365

In Job's search for God amid his pain, he feels that God is distant, seemingly hidden in his suffering. Yet, in Matthew 12, we see Jesus bringing God's love and power to those who seek Him, revealing God's heart through His words and actions. It is the Holy Spirit who opens our eyes to recognize God's work and to sense His nearness, even when circumstances suggest otherwise.

The Spirit is our constant guide, especially in trials, helping us trust that God is present, attentive, and loving. When we are willing to lean into the Spirit's presence, we find comfort and clarity even in uncertainty.

Today, ask the Holy Spirit to make you aware of God's presence. Trust that He is near, working within and around you to provide the strength you need.

Today's Readings:
Job 22 • Job 23 • Job 24
Matthew 12:1-23

S.O.A.P

SCRIPTURE:

_____
_____
_____
_____
_____
_____
_____

OBSERVATION:

_____
_____
_____
_____
_____
_____
_____
_____
_____
_____
_____
_____
_____

APPLICATION:

PRAYER:

JANUARY 18
DAY 18 OF 365

Job insists on his integrity, committing not to let his lips speak falsehood or deceit. Jesus reminds us in Matthew 12 that our words reveal the condition of our hearts, saying that the mouth speaks from the abundance of the heart. The Holy Spirit works within us to cultivate a heart that reflects God's love and truth, transforming our words to align with His character.

As we yield to the Spirit, He helps us speak life, encouragement, and wisdom to those around us. Our words become a reflection of His work in us, drawing others toward God.

Today, invite the Spirit to shape your words and purify your heart. Let your speech be filled with grace and truth, allowing God's love to shine through you.

Today's Readings:
Job 25 • Job 26 • Job 27
Matthew 12:24-50

S.O.A.P

SCRIPTURE:

OBSERVATION:

APPLICATION:

PRAYER:

JANUARY 19
DAY 19 OF 365

In Job 28, Job recognizes that true wisdom belongs to God alone and that human understanding is limited. Jesus, in Matthew 13, uses parables to teach about the mysteries of God's kingdom, revealing truths that only the Spirit can help us understand. The Holy Spirit gives us insight, opening our hearts and minds to divine wisdom that goes beyond human knowledge.

As we listen to the Spirit, He guides us in discerning truth, helping us live with purpose and understanding. God's wisdom is a gift, one that enables us to navigate life with clarity and peace.

Today, seek the Spirit's guidance in every area of your life. Ask Him to grant you wisdom that comes only from God, leading you to walk in His truth.

Today's Readings:
Job 28 • Job 29
Matthew 13:1-30

S.O.A.P

SCRIPTURE:

OBSERVATION:

APPLICATION:

PRAYER:

JANUARY 20
DAY 20 OF 365

Job laments the drastic changes in his life, unable to understand his suffering. Meanwhile, Jesus speaks in parables, illustrating how God's kingdom often grows in unexpected ways. The Holy Spirit helps us see God's purpose in every season, even when we don't fully understand it.

During times of difficulty, the Spirit reassures us that God is working, using each season to shape and refine us. His purpose may not always be visible, but we can trust that He is faithful in all things.

Today, invite the Holy Spirit to give you peace in your current season. Allow Him to deepen your trust, knowing that God is always at work in ways you may not yet see.

Today's Readings:
Job 30 • Job 31
Matthew 13:31-58

S.O.A.P

SCRIPTURE:

___

OBSERVATION:

___

APPLICATION:

PRAYER:

JANUARY 21
DAY 21 OF 365

Job's friend Elihu believes God speaks in subtle ways, through whispers or quiet dreams. In Matthew 14, Jesus withdraws to a solitary place, seeking communion with the Father in stillness. The Holy Spirit often speaks to us in these quiet moments, offering guidance, encouragement, and peace that refreshes our souls.

When we create space for stillness, we become more sensitive to the Spirit's voice, finding clarity and wisdom. He invites us to pause, listen, and experience God's presence in the quiet.

Today, take time to be still before God. Let the Spirit speak to you, trusting that His voice will bring the wisdom and encouragement you need.

Today's Readings:
Job 32 • Job 33
Matthew 14:1-21

S.O.A.P

SCRIPTURE:

OBSERVATION:

APPLICATION:

PRAYER:

JANUARY 22
DAY 22 OF 365

In Matthew 14, Peter steps out of the boat to walk on water toward Jesus. When fear takes hold, he begins to sink, but Jesus reaches out to save him. Like Peter, we often need courage to step out in faith. The Holy Spirit strengthens us, reminding us to keep our eyes on Jesus and helping us overcome fear.

The Spirit empowers us to take bold steps even when life feels uncertain, and He redirects our focus to God's presence rather than our circumstances. With the Spirit, we can step into the unknown with confidence.

Today, invite the Holy Spirit to give you courage for whatever lies ahead. Keep your gaze fixed on Jesus, trusting Him to hold you steady as you move forward in faith.

Today's Readings:
Job 34 • Job 35
Matthew 14:22-36

S.O.A.P

SCRIPTURE:

OBSERVATION:

APPLICATION:

_____

PRAYER:

_____

JANUARY 23
DAY 23 OF 365

In Job 36-37, Elihu describes God's greatness and purity, emphasizing His power and holiness. He reminds Job of God's might and the awe we should have for Him, a God who controls the skies and the seasons. In Matthew 15, Jesus teaches that what defiles a person is not what goes into the mouth, but what comes out of the heart, for our words and actions reveal our true nature.

The Holy Spirit works within us to cultivate this purity of heart that Jesus speaks of, transforming our desires and aligning them with God's character. When we surrender to the Spirit, He cleanses our hearts and enables us to live lives that reflect God's holiness and love.

Today, ask the Spirit to reveal any areas in your heart that need cleansing. Invite Him to purify your intentions, so that your words and actions reflect the purity and holiness of God, drawing others closer to Him.

Today's Readings:
Job 36 • Job 37
Matthew 15:1-20

S.O.A.P

SCRIPTURE:

OBSERVATION:

APPLICATION:

PRAYER:

JANUARY 24
DAY 24 OF 365

In Job 38-40, God speaks to Job from the storm, revealing His power over creation and reminding Job of His authority. The Holy Spirit opens our eyes to this same awe, helping us perceive God's majesty in the world around us. From the vastness of the seas to the intricacies of each creature, the Spirit reveals God's hand at work.

In Matthew 15, we see Jesus's compassion and power as He heals and feeds thousands, reminding us that this powerful Creator is also deeply compassionate. The Spirit invites us to see both God's greatness and His tender care.

Today, ask the Holy Spirit to help you marvel at God's works, seeing His power and compassion in everything around you.

Today's Readings:
Job 38 • Job 39 • Job 40
Matthew 15:21-39

S.O.A.P

SCRIPTURE:

OBSERVATION:

APPLICATION:

PRAYER:

JANUARY 25
DAY 25 OF 365

The end of Job's story is a powerful reminder of God's restoration. After his trials, God blesses Job with renewed health, family, and possessions, demonstrating His compassion. The Holy Spirit is the one who brings this restoration into our own lives, healing us and renewing our hearts.

In Matthew 16, Jesus speaks of building His church, declaring that even the gates of hell will not prevail against it. Just as God restored Job, the Spirit strengthens and restores us, enabling us to stand firm in God's promises.

Today, ask the Holy Spirit to bring renewal and healing to any area in need of restoration. Trust that God's power to restore is at work in your life.

Today's Readings:
Job 41 • Job 42
Matthew 16

S.O.A.P

SCRIPTURE:

OBSERVATION:

APPLICATION:

PRAYER:

JANUARY 26
DAY 26 OF 365

In Genesis 24, Abraham's servant prays for guidance in finding a wife for Isaac, trusting God to lead him with clarity. God answers his prayer, bringing Rebekah to him in a way that demonstrates His precise guidance and care. The Holy Spirit works similarly in our lives, guiding us toward God's purposes and preparing our way, often beyond what we can see.

In Matthew 17, the disciples witness Jesus's transfiguration, catching a glimpse of His divine glory. The Spirit opens our eyes to this same majesty and provision, helping us perceive God's presence in both miraculous and ordinary moments. He reassures us that God is actively involved in our journey.

Today, ask the Holy Spirit to direct your path and to help you see God's hand at work around you. Trust that He will provide what you need and lead you toward God's purposes, even when the way forward is unclear.

Today's Readings:
Genesis 23 • Genesis 24
Matthew 17

S.O.A.P

SCRIPTURE:

OBSERVATION:

APPLICATION:

_____
_____
_____
_____
_____
_____
_____
_____
_____
_____

PRAYER:

_____
_____
_____
_____
_____
_____
_____
_____
_____
_____
_____
_____
_____

JANUARY 27
DAY 27 OF 365

In Matthew 18, Jesus teaches His disciples that greatness in God's kingdom comes through humility, encouraging them to be like little children. The Holy Spirit nurtures this humility in our hearts, reminding us to approach God and others with gentleness and openness.

In Genesis 26, Isaac shows humility by moving away from conflict over wells, trusting God to provide for him elsewhere. The Spirit empowers us to choose peace and humility, teaching us that our security is in God's hands.

Today, ask the Holy Spirit to cultivate a humble heart in you. Let Him guide your responses and remind you that true greatness lies in serving others and trusting God's provision.

Today's Readings:
Genesis 25 • Genesis 26
Matthew 18:1-20

S.O.A.P

SCRIPTURE:

OBSERVATION:

APPLICATION:

PRAYER:

JANUARY 28
DAY 28 OF 365

In Matthew 18, Jesus calls us to forgive others without limit, just as God has forgiven us. The Holy Spirit enables us to forgive when it feels difficult, reminding us of the grace we have received. Through the Spirit, we find the strength to release bitterness and walk in freedom.

Genesis 27-28 tells of Jacob's deception and the consequences that follow. Despite Jacob's actions, God extends grace to him, demonstrating His faithfulness. The Spirit empowers us to extend this same grace to others, freeing us to forgive and move forward.

Today, ask the Holy Spirit to help you forgive any unresolved hurt. Allow Him to guide you in extending grace, knowing that forgiveness leads to freedom.

Today's Readings:
Genesis 27 • Genesis 28
Matthew 18:21-35

S.O.A.P

SCRIPTURE:

OBSERVATION:

APPLICATION:

PRAYER:

JANUARY 29
DAY 29 OF 365

In Genesis 29-30, Jacob endures years of hardship and disappointment as he works for Laban. Despite his struggles, God is present, blessing Jacob with a growing family and fulfilling His promise to Abraham. Even in difficult and messy circumstances, God's plan is unfolding, and He is preparing Jacob for something greater. The Holy Spirit reminds us of this same truth—that God is at work in our lives, weaving together a story that often looks different from what we expect.

In Matthew 19, Jesus teaches about God's design for relationships, calling us to align our lives with His purposes. The Spirit guides us in this process, helping us trust that God's plans are good and that He is faithful to accomplish His work in us, even when the path is challenging.

Today, ask the Holy Spirit to help you see God's hand in your own journey. Trust that He is present in every season, and let Him guide you as you align your life with God's purposes, knowing that His plan is always unfolding.

Today's Readings:
Genesis 29 • Genesis 30
Matthew 19

S.O.A.P

SCRIPTURE:

_____
_____
_____
_____
_____
_____
_____
_____

OBSERVATION:

_____
_____
_____
_____
_____
_____
_____
_____
_____
_____
_____
_____
_____
_____

APPLICATION:

PRAYER:

JANUARY 30
DAY 30 OF 365

In Genesis 31-32, Jacob prepares to meet his estranged brother, Esau, by offering gifts as a gesture of peace. This act of generosity reflects his humility and desire for reconciliation, showing that sometimes the greatest gifts come from a transformed heart. The Holy Spirit works within us to cultivate this kind of generosity, leading us to release pride and approach others with grace and humility.

In Matthew 20, Jesus's parable of the vineyard workers illustrates God's boundless generosity and mercy, reminding us that His blessings are not given based on our merit but on His love. The Spirit encourages us to mirror God's generosity, not clinging tightly to what we have but freely giving to others as He leads.

Today, ask the Holy Spirit to help you approach others with a generous and humble heart. Allow Him to guide you to give freely, knowing that God has been endlessly generous with you.

Today's Readings:
Genesis 31 • Genesis 32
Matthew 20:1-16

S.O.A.P

SCRIPTURE:

OBSERVATION:

APPLICATION:

_____
_____
_____
_____
_____
_____
_____
_____

PRAYER:

_____
_____
_____
_____
_____
_____
_____
_____
_____
_____
_____

JANUARY 31
DAY 31 OF 365

In Genesis 33, Jacob humbly meets Esau, seeking reconciliation after years of estrangement. Jacob's act of surrender paves the way for restored relationship, showing how God's purposes can unfold when we let go of our pride. The Holy Spirit empowers us to live in this same posture of surrender, aligning our desires with God's will rather than our own agendas.

In Matthew 20, Jesus tells His disciples about His coming sacrifice, exemplifying a life fully surrendered to God's plan. The Spirit guides us into this type of submission, teaching us to trust God's wisdom even when His plans lead us into unknown or uncomfortable territory.

Today, invite the Holy Spirit to help you surrender areas where you're holding back. Ask Him to lead you in aligning your heart with God's purposes, trusting that His will is always good.

Today's Readings:
Genesis 33 • Genesis 34 • Genesis 35
Matthew 20:17-34

S.O.A.P

SCRIPTURE:

OBSERVATION:

APPLICATION:

PRAYER: